Easy desserts for beginners

Lactose-free desserts recipes

Table of contents

Waffle Cones 3

Citrus Muffins 5

Meringue Roulade 7

Chocolate Meringue Roulade 10

Fruit Fantasy Cake 14

Nutella 20

Banana Oatmeal Cookies 23

Peanut Cookies 25

Caramel Ice Cream 27

Raspberry sorbet 30

Profiteroles 32

Waffle Cones

Your future cones will be tasty and crispy. The recipe is adapted for lactose intolerant people.

Ingredients:
- 1 Egg (55 g)
- Sugar - 160 g
- Vanilla
- Pinch of salt
- Water/milk – 30 g
- Vegetable oil - 30 g
- Flour - 70 g

The recipe contains water, but you can use lactose-free milk, nut milk — everything to your taste and preferences.

You will need:

Bowl, whisk, waffle iron, cone roller.

Directions:

1. In a bowl, whisk together the egg, vanilla, salt, and sugar until the mixture is combined.
2. While whisking add water. Next, vegetable oil (take something that does not have a strong taste and smell, such as grape seed oil).
3. Add flour. Combine all the ingredients. The dough will be a bit thicker than for the pancakes.
4. Heat the waffle iron. One tablespoon will be enough for one cone — Cook the waffle.
5. We shape the cones right away, as soon as they are ready. Otherwise, they will not be able to turn into a cone.

Citrus Muffins

Ingredients:
- Tangerines - 400 g
- 6 eggs
- Almond flour - 200 g
- Cocoa - 50 g
- Sugar - 200 g
- Baking powder - 8 g
- Baking soda - 4 g
- Salt - 2 g

Directions:
1. Scald tangerines with boiling water. This will remove bitterness from the peel.

2. Put tangerines in a saucepan, pour boiling water, put on a slow fire and cook for 2 hours. Drain, let the tangerines cool. Divide the tangerines into pieces, get the seeds out of it — grind tangerines with a blender.
3. Preheat oven to 180 ° C.
4. Transfer the tangerine puree to the mixer bowl, add eggs and granulated sugar to them, whisk.
5. Add dry ingredients (almond flour, cocoa, soda, baking powder, soda) to the tangerine mixture. Mix until smooth.
6. Grease muffin molds with coconut oil and sprinkle with flour. Put the dough in the prepared molds.
7. Bake the muffin in the oven until it is cooked. Approximately it will take 40-45 minutes.
8. When the muffins have cooled, remove it from the mold.

Enjoy your meal. As an addition, you can pour muffins with tangerine syrup.

Merinque Roulade

This dessert has already conquered many. Soft, light dessert, and surprisingly not sugary sweet with a slight sourness of strawberries.

Ingredients for roulade:
- 5 Egg whites (275 g)
- Sugar – 220 g
- Pinch of salt
- Lemon juice – 1 tsp

Ingredients for cream:
- Coconut cream - 200 ml
- Sugar powder
- Strawberry – 100 g
- Pistachio nuts

You will need:
Mixer, bowl, parchment paper, spatula

Directions:
1. In the bowl, we combine egg whites, sugar, salt, and lemon juice. Beat everything at maximum speed until stiff.
2. Put the meringue on a parchment-laid baking sheet. Smooth with a spatula or spoon. The layer thickness is approximately 1.5 cm.
3. Bake in the preheated oven to 175 C or 350 F for 20-25 minutes. When baking, do not open.
4. Remove from the oven. Leave to cool, turn on a towel or other sheet of parchment, remove the paper from the meringue.

5. While the meringue cools, make the cream. Beat cream with powdered sugar. Dice strawberries and nuts.

6. On a cooled meringue apply the cream, sprinkle with strawberries and pistachios. Twist the roll. Transfer to a dish and refrigerate for 40-60 minutes to soak.

After cooling, chop and serve. Bon Appetit.

Chocolate Merinque Roulade

This roulade is an option on the use of dry albumin powder, for those who do not like to use raw egg whites. You can also use the roulade from the previous recipe.

Ingredients for roulade:
- Albumin - 16 g
- Water - 130 g
- Sugar powder - 200 g
- Vanilla - 8 g
- Cocoa - 2 tbsp

Ingredients for cream:

- Coconut cream - 200 ml
- Sugar powder - 80 g
- Cocoa - 20 g

Directions:

1. Add some water to albumin and mix. Pour the remaining liquid until it is completely dissolved. Leave for 10 minutes, during this time albumin will get into a reaction with water and will be suitable for beating.
2. Pour the recovered proteins into the mixer bowl and start to beat with a mixer at medium speed until all the bubbles are the same (like beer foam). Now, start adding a spoonful of powdered sugar. Added a spoon, 5 seconds, and the next one. At the same time, increase the speed to the maximum! And so on until all the powder is over.
3. Beat to dense peaks. The mass should be elastic and shiny.

4. Add cocoa and with a spatula knead the mass from the bottom up. Do not knead for a long time!
5. Next, put parchment on a baking sheet, grease it with vegetable oil, pour the meringue, and spread it thickly.
6. Put in the oven preheated to 160C and bake for 12-13 minutes. Then turn off the oven and hold the baking sheet there for another 5 minutes. (Do not open the door!)
7. Take out the baking sheet. Take another one sheet of parchment. Put it on top of our meringue and turn it over. We remove the paper from the inverted side and leave our cake until it cools completely.

Directions for cream:

1. Beat coconut cream with powdered sugar to medium peaks. Begin to beat at a slow speed, gradually increase to medium.

2. When the cream is fluffy, add the cocoa powder and mix gently until smooth.
3. Carefully coat the meringue biscuit. Add on top of the cream, if you want crushed nuts. Twist the roulade.
4. Transfer to a dish, decorate and put in the fridge for 40-60 minutes.

Enjoy your meal.

Fruit Fantasy Cake

Lactose-free cake for those who have an intolerance to cow protein and lactose. If you change the wheat flour in the sponge cake to rice flour, then the cake can be made as gluten-free. The product comes out fluffy, fragrant, and very tasty. Both children and adults like it; even those who are accustomed to regular baking like this recipe.

D **-20 cm**

Weight **-1.800 kg**

Ingredients for sponge cake:

- 5 eggs - 275 g
- Sugar - 190 g
- Wheat flour - 200 g
- Baking powder - 5 g
- Pinch of salt

Lemon-pear curd:

- 2 pears - 330 g
- Sugar - 60 g
- Lemon juice - 40 g
- Lemon zest
- 2 egg yolks 40 g
- Starch - 10 g
- Water 30 g (30 ml = 2 tbsp)

Caramelized apple

- 4 Apples (strain Golden) - 670 g
- Sugar - 100 g
- Lemon juice - 30 g (30 ml = 2 tbsp)
- Cinnamon - 4 g (1 tsp)

Cream filling (Italian meringue)

- 2 Egg whites - 60 g
- Lemon juice
- Pinch of salt
- Sugar - 120 g
- Water - 60 g

Mostly for the cream filling I use vegetable coconut creams. I just mix it with a sugar powder for the desired consistency and cover the cooled cake.

Directions:

Sponge cake

1. Preheat the oven to 180 C.
2. Cover the bottom of the mold with a diameter of 20 cm parchment paper
3. It is not required to grease the sides.
4. Sieve flour 1-2 times.
5. In the blender bowl, we mix eggs and powdered sugar. Whip the mass at the

medium speed until stiff. Carefully, with the help of the spatula, mix flour with baking powder.

6. Pour the dough into the mold and bake 40 minutes until it is ready.
7. Cool the cake. It is best to cover it with the food film and place in the refrigerator for 6-8 hours. It will moisturize the cake evenly, so it will not be crunchy when you cut it.
8. Cut it in 4 layers.

Lemon-pear curd

1. Peel the pears and the core out of it, cut and grind with the blender to the puree.
2. Add sugar, lemon juice, zest, egg yolks and starch diluted with water.
3. Cook the mass on low heat in a saucepan with a thick bottom, stirring with a whisk
4. While the curd is hot, sieve it through the sieve to get rid of hard pear particles, lemon zest. Transfer into the dish for cooling, cover

with the film. Leave at room temperature for cooling.

Caramelized apples

1. Clean the apples, cut into the pieces (about 1 cm per 1 cm) and put it in a saucepan with the thick bottom.
2. Add sugar, lemon juice, cinnamon and on a slow fire, stew to the softness of the apples.
3. Cool.
4. Using apples strain Golden, while caramelizing it will not fall apart and remains pieces. Lemon juice will allow them to save a light shade.

Meringue

1. In the saucepan, pour the water and add powdered sugar. Put on fire and cook to t 118 c.
2. If you do not have a thermometer, boil the syrup until it is viscous.

3. In clean and dry dishes, to the soft peaks, whip the egg whites, salt, and lemon juice.
4. While whipping at the medium speed, slowly add hot syrup.
5. Increase the speed and continue whipping until the meringue is cold and stiff.

Assembling

Sponge cake - Curd – Sponge cake - caramelized apples – Sponge cake - Curd – Sponge cake

To assemble the cake, you will need the substrate of the desired diameter, in the form of the ring. Cover inside of the ring with a curb ribbon, acetate film. It is best to assemble and place it for 4 hours in the cold to firm it up. This will make the layers less likely to slide around as you work, and the cake won't shed crumbs as you frost.

Nutella

We need a very powerful blender! Because you can grind nuts for a long time and blender can be spoiled. But this Nutella is more delicious than the bought one and more healthy. It can be prepared without using sugar or replace sugar with the sweetener, and it will be a healthy nutrition product.

Ingredients:

- Hazelnut – 350 g
- Sugar powder – 80 g

- Cocoa – 40 g
- Coconut oil – 20 g
- Pinch of salt
- Vanilla sugar

Directions:

1. Heat the oven to 160 C. Spread the hazelnuts in a single layer on a baking sheet and toast them in the oven until they've browned a little and the skins are blistered a little.
2. Remove the tray, let the nuts cool. Clean if you did not purchase originally blanched.
3. Put the nuts in the blender bowl. Grind until they form a paste. Next add to our hazelnut mass: salt, vanilla sugar, coconut oil, sugar powder, cocoa.
4. You will need the patience to do this step. Continue to grind until the nuts produce oil; it will make the mixture smooth and tasty. The mass will heat up while grinding, so don't be frightened.

5. Scrape the mass in the jar and store in a cool place or refrigerator. In the cold, it will become denser and will quickly become a Nutella at its finest.

Bon Appetit.

Banana Oatmeal Cookies

In the recipe is used oat-flakes, if you use oatmeal flour texture of the cookies will become more tender.

Ingredients:
- 2 Bananas (350 g)
- Honey – 1 tbsp
- Oat-flakes – 200 g
- Walnuts – 100 g
- Cinnamon – ¼ tsp
- Pinch of salt

Directions:

1. Preheat the oven to 180C
2. Mash bananas with the fork. Add oat - flakes, mix until it is combined. Add honey and mix again.
3. Chop walnuts with the knife. Add it to the mashed bananas and oat – flakes.
4. And the last one, add salt and cinnamon, mix again.
5. Cover the baking sheet with the parchment paper.
6. Put our cookies on the baking sheet with the spoon; let it set in.
7. Bake in the oven for 15-20 minutes. The baking time depends on the type of your oven.
8. Take the cookies out of the oven. Let it cool.

Bon Appetit.

Peanut Cookies

Ingredients:
- Peanut - 180 g
- Cocoa oil- 165 g
- 1 Egg
- Sugar - 140 g
- Flour - 300 g
- Baking powder - 4 g
- Baking soda - 4 g
- Salt - 2 g

Directions:
1. Heat the oven to 160C. Put peanuts on a dry baking sheet. Bake it until golden brown. Peel

if necessary. It is more convenient to buy already peeled. Let it cool. Grind with a rolling pin or knife.
2. Preheat the oven to 180 C. Cover the baking sheet with the parchment paper.
3. Mix in the bowl mix coconut oil, egg, and sugar until it is combined.
4. In another bowl mix baking powder, baking soda, salt, and flour. Pour it into the oil-egg mixture, mix until smooth. Add crushed peanuts and knead again.
5. Roll the balls from the dough approximately 30 grams. Put the balls on the parchment. Press down the cookies with a fork. Bake cookies for 15 minutes until it is golden. It is important not to overbake the cookies in the oven. Firstly, cookies will be soft, but after cooling, it becomes solid and crunchy.

Bon Appetit.

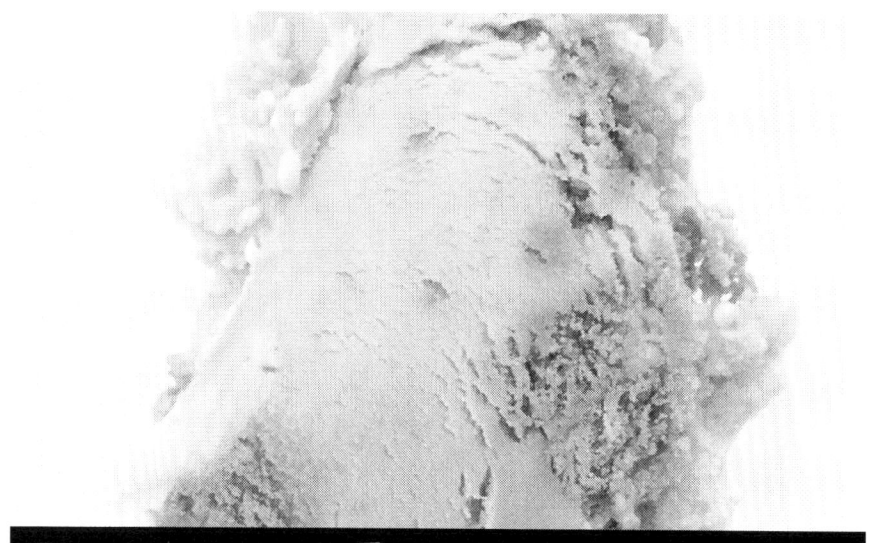

Caramel Ice Cream

Ingredients for caramel sauce:

- Sugar - 90 g
- Coconut heavy cream - 180 g
- Salt - 2 g (1/1tsp)

Ingredients for English cream:

- Coconut heavy cream - 320 g
- Coconut milk - 180 g
- Sugar - 60 g
- 5 egg yolks (100 g)

Directions for caramel sauce:

1. Take the saucepan, add sugar, heat the sugar until it is melted. Wait until it turns gold. Then pour preheated heavy cream.
2. Stir it with the wooden spatula until it is smooth. When the caramel is ready, add salt and mix it.

Directions for English cream:

1. Combine egg yolks with sugar.
2. In a saucepan, mix the milk with the cream, bring to a boil. Pour on yolks stirring with a whisk. When the mixture merges, pour it back into the saucepan and put on a slow fire.
3. Constantly stirring with a whisk, bring the mixture to a temperature of 80-85 C. By that time, the dough should already thicken. Blend the resulting mass into a smooth texture. Stir in the caramel sauce, smash again with a blender until smooth. Cool to room temperature.

4. Transfer the future ice cream to a plastic container with a lid, place in the freezer for 30 minutes. Beat the ice cream with a mixer, once again place the ice cream in the freezer. Repeat the procedure 3-4 times.

Serve the ice cream in waffle cones, pour it with the caramel sauce, if you want you can sprinkle it with the nuts.

If you want to create a variation of ice cream, instead of caramel cream, you can add peanut butter, Nutella, berry or fruit puree to the English cream, add mashed banana.

Enjoy your meal.

Raspberry Sorbet

This recipe is the base for any berry or fruit sorbet. Your fantasy is unlimited. You can make one flavored sorbet or combine different flavors.

Ingredients:

- Fresh raspberry - 250 g
- Sugar - 70 g
- Lemon juice - 20 g
- Corn starch - 10 g
- Water - 250 g

Directions:

1. Grind raspberry with blender, sieve with a sieve. Seeds that remained in the sieve transfer to a saucepan add to them 220 gram of water and sugar. Put on fire, boil the syrup for 2-3 minutes. Strain the syrup again through a sieve, remove the pulp from the seed.
2. Strained syrup pours into a saucepan, add lemon juice. Dissolve starch in 30 grams of water. When the syrup boils, pour starch into it with water. When the syrup thickens, remove from heat and cool.
3. Mix the syrup with raspberry puree, put it in a plastic container, cover with a lid, send it to the freezer. After 30 minutes, beat the raspberry sorbet with a mixer. Repeat the procedure 3-4 times.

After 2-3 hours you have a delicious sorbet. Enjoy your meal.

Profiteroles

French dessert that everybody loves. The main thing - you can fill profiteroles with different creams and get a variety of desserts.

Ingredients for the dough:
- Coconut oil - 100 g
- Water - 250 g
- Sugar - 10 g
- Salt - 5 g
- Flour - 150 g
- 5 Eggs

All ingredients should be room temperature; then you get the right combination.

Ingredients for the cream:
- Coconut milk - 500 g
- Vanilla - 1 stick
- Sugar - 100 g
- 2 Eggs (110 g) or 4 egg yolks (100 g)
- Corn starch - 30 g
- Grinded hazelnut - 100 g

Directions:
1. In a saucepan, combine coconut oil, water, sugar, and salt. Boil. When the mixture boils, pour the flour, stirring slowly not removing from the heat. The dough should stick together in a ball.
2. Put the dough in the bowl of the mixer. Beat with mixer and add eggs until it is combined.
3. Put the dough in a pastry bag with a round nozzle. Fill the future profiteroles in a

checkerboard pattern on a baking sheet covered with parchment paper for good air circulation. The diameter of profiteroles should be about 1 cm, the distance between profiteroles is about 3 cm. Profiteroles need space to grow.
4. Turn the oven to 220C. At this temperature, we bake profiteroles for 15 minutes, without opening the oven door, reduce the heat in the oven to 180C and bake profiteroles to a golden brown, for about 15-20 minutes.

If you open the oven before the profiteroles are fully baked, they will settle.

Directions for cream:
1. Mix yolks with sugar.
2. Pour the milk and the vanilla seeds into a saucepan, bring it to a boil. Pour the mixture on yolks stirring with a whisk. When the

mixture is combined, pour it back into the pan and put on a slow fire.

3. Constantly stirring with a whisk, bring the mixture to a temperature of 80-85 C. By that time, the dough should be already thickened. Blend the mass into a smooth texture. Mix cream with chopped hazelnuts. Cool it down.

Fill profiteroles with cream. Enjoy your meal.

Printed in Great Britain
by Amazon